HOW TO BUILD "KINGDOM MINDED" ORGANIZATIONS

Good News for Tumultuous Times: Giving Your Employees a Hope and a Future in This Upside Down World

Mark A. Griffin

ISBN: 0615617514

ISBN-13: 978-0615617510

DEDICATION

I dedicate this book to my family. To Gail, my beautiful and inspirational wife, thank you for the support you have provided me for 26 years to become the man I am. To Adam, thank you for all the love and excitement you have given us. Your spirit and love for life is contagious. To Emily, I thank you for your inspiration in your encouragement to share the message of Jesus with all who will listen. As for me and my house, we will serve the Lord.

God * Family * Education

MARK A. GRIFFIN

INTRODUCTION

We each have our own way of sharing our faith. Sometimes you meet people whom you admire because they present their faith in such an inviting and respectful manner. That is the core mission of this book that you hold in your hands.

As Christians, we are called to share the Gospel. As a Christian leader in the marketplace or nonprofit, you have an unique opportunity in which to do this. My desire is to help you create a voice of truth in your organization that will encourage your people while being fully respectful of their beliefs — a voice of truth that will serve as the pillar of the *Mission, Vision, and Values* of your organization.

I became a Christian while working in a secular company, and I soon discovered that it was not a good fit for me. Hiding my faith while working as an HR executive was just not possible, yet it was a requirement in our "politically correct" corporation.

I then spent seven years praying, writing, navigating, and experimenting with implementing Christianity in the workplace at the last two Christian-owned companies in which I led HR. What I found was startling. Where I thought faith would be obvious, it was not. Where I thought there would be offerings of spiritual guidance for employees, I found it vacant. Where I thought I would find a desire to grow the Kingdom through the company's employees and on out into their communities, and ultimately supporting church growth, I found it haphazard and without a plan.

After spending many years in high performing *Fortune*-ranked companies, I developed methods to help drive employees to excellence, and designed world-class human resource programs and processes. During my last two years working as a vice president of human resources, I took this further. I developed a model which took my past experiences and discoveries in the art of human resources and wove them together with my faith. This model – the focus of this book – is how I believe God would like us to lead our organizations as Christians.

The end result has been nothing less than astonishing and gratifying. Every time I explain my approach to a leader, that leader grows eager to know more. In April of 2011 I set out on another journey: taking my model and message to the world. The first two steps were to grow my network and then provide encouragement to that network. God rewarded me by enabling me to use technology to reach countless people in so many areas of the world. Less than one year later, with more than twenty-five hundred Facebook fans, thirty thousand Twitter followers and over seventeen hundred LinkedIn connections lined up and waiting, I present to you this model for building Kingdom Minded Organizations.

CONTENTS

ACKNOWLEDGMENTS

There are so many people and so many organizations that I appreciate. To my loving wife who truly encouraged me to live out my heart- I love you. To my father James A. Griffin, thank you for the education you provided me. It has been my rock and my foundation. To Pastor Powell-thank you for speaking the good news into me back in 2003. To Pastor Ashcraft thank you for keeping the fire alive in me and your constant reminder to always think "others" first. To Jimmy Nimon — Thank you for keeping me focused in my prayer life and helping me find that one last piece to turn over to God, you are awesome. To Paul Jaspers, thank you for being my best friend and challenging me when I needed it. And finally to Alan Collins, your support has been immeasurable. Thank you for your encouragement!

MARK A. GRIFFIN

PART ONE

1. WHY YOU NEED FAITH IN THE WORKPLACE

Today's churches sit empty. <u>More than any other time in history,</u> your employees spend increased amounts of time commuting to and from work and working evenings and weekends, disengaged from their families and communities. Increased hours and workloads have resulted in employees spending more waking hours at work than they spend at home with their families and friends or volunteering in their communities. Because of this, we have an opportunity and a mission: reach those who need saving. This is the world's <u>untapped harvest, a vast field of opportunity for those in the Body of Christ.</u> And, as God proclaims, we need more workers in His fields.

> *Matthew 9: 35-38 (NIV)* **The Workers Are Few**[35] *Jesus went through all the towns and villages, teaching in their synagogues, proclaiming the good news of the kingdom and healing every disease and sickness.*[36] *When He saw the crowds, He had compassion on them, because they were harassed and helpless, like sheep without a shepherd.*[37] *Then He said to his disciples, "The harvest is plentiful but the workers are few.*[38] *Ask the Lord of the harvest, therefore, to send out workers into His harvest field."*

According to a December 2008 Gallup poll, 42 percent of US residents — about 128 million Americans — claim to attend religious services at least once every week. This number is probably misleading because many people may embellish their attendance out of a sense of guilt or obligation. However, assuming it is accurate, that still leaves a <u>whopping 58 percent of U.S. residents</u> who do not attend church. This is a concern because it indicates that your employees are probably not spiritually grounded.

This is where Christian business owners and executives must step in to help God fill the void.

As a human resources professional with 20 years of experience in both public and private organizations, I can tell you from firsthand experience that this lack of faith has a huge affect on the workplace. Employees' lack of time to focus on their spiritual needs will undoubtedly affect productivity, quality, and safety. Harder to measure but just as important, it affects each employee's morale. Employees lacking in faith will bring more problems to the workplace than those who seek God or are Christ followers.

You can try to run your business without God.

Or you can include Him in your plans.

I urge you to include Him.

God is the ultimate business partner!

Those of us who are hesitant to embrace Christianity in the workplace must look at it not only from a spiritual perspective but also from a business perspective. Far from being self-serving, this conveys the responsible attitude of a business owner attempting to prosper their business for the financial security and future of their employees and employees' families.

Makes Financial Sense

Leading an organization with Christ-centered values just makes good business sense. I believe that Christ-centered organizations can experience:

- Lower absenteeism
- Higher quality products
- Fewer employee morale issues
- Safer work environments
- Better perceptions by customers and vendors

What I Have Found to Work

Your organization must have a Mission, Vision, and Core Values. Later in this book I'll refer to this as MVV and explain those in detail. But many business professionals stop there. I urge all of you to go further by integrating your *Mission, Vision, and Core Values* into your Human Resources practices. This will:

- Memorialize your standards
- Provide guiding principles in all you do
- Make your values easily understood by employees
- Drive a values-based culture with your customers

I believe that employees who work for an outwardly faith-based, Christian organization are committed at a different level than those in non-faith-based organizations. Employees are more likely to go the extra mile, to trust their leadership, to deliver on their promises, and be led by those who demonstrate Christ-like servant leadership, because they can!

2. WHAT IS A "KINGDOM MINDED" ORGANIZATION?

When I meet with people to talk about bettering their HR practices, I use the term "Kingdom Minded" organization. More often than not they are <u>intrigued by the terminology</u> I use in reference to helping them build their organizations. Many Christian business people, pastors and Christian business consultants have their own opinions or definitions of what a "Kingdom Minded" organization is.

I have developed what I believe is a fairly <u>clear, actionable and measurable</u> way to articulate what a "Kingdom Minded" organization is, thus inspiring business owners to invest their time, financial resources, and energy into making their organization prosperous and reflective of Christ. So, let me begin by outlining what comprises the framework when building a "Kingdom Minded" organization.

Throughout this book, I will walk us through a more in-depth look at each piece of the framework. I will ask you to <u>look internally at what you believe</u> your "Kingdom Minded Purpose" is for your organization. In building a "Kingdom Minded" organization, the model I developed contains the following ingredients, listed in order of importance.

These same principles that apply to marketplace businesses apply to non-profit organizations as well.

A "Kingdom Minded" organization:

- Puts Christ First
- Has a Clear Mission
- Has a Clear Vision
- Has Core Values

Has agreed upon Goals and Objectives, especially in:

- Safety
- Production
- Quality
- Customer Service

And finally, a "Kingdom Minded" organization strives for prosperity for the good of its owners, employees, and the organization's community. If you want to enjoy prosperity, you must look inward and address these critical aspects of running your organization.

Take a look inside your own organization. Do you have a mission? A vision? Core values? How are you with setting or receiving expectations through organization goals and objectives? Do you collectively work together as a team for <u>success and prosperity</u>?

Having spent over 20 years in HR I can tell you organizations that have a well-developed and bought-in *Mission, Vision and Values* will far exceed those who do not.

PART TWO

SEVEN PREMISES FOR "KINGDOM MINDED" ORGANIZATION-BUILDING SUCCESS

As we navigate through our lives, our experiences inevitably shape us. We have good jobs and bad jobs, excellent bosses and not so excellent bosses. We work for good organizations and terrible organizations. If you are like me, you have worked in organizations where you felt taken advantage of, unappreciated, and undervalued. But, then again, you have probably worked for an organization where you felt fulfilled and valued and worked to your peak potential.

I have been blessed to have had my fair share of employment experiences across industries, across varying organization sizes and structures, from publicly traded Fortune 500s to modest, privately held organizations. I have also been fortunate to coach thousands of job seekers who have lost jobs either through no fault of their own or were fired. These experiences have created an incredible bank of knowledge and experiences upon which I rely. I have had many key learning experiences from my various adventures (or what some may describe as misadventures).

Having had all of these experiences in both secular and Christian-owned organizations, as well as Christian nonprofits, I have encountered "readiness" levels within organizations signaling whether or not the organization was ready and capable of becoming "Kingdom Minded." Unfortunately, and it may not come as any great surprise to you, I have witnessed organizations who pompously proclaim their righteousness and holiness when they had no right to do so. This is not the same thing as being a Kingdom Minded organization! Yes, I have witnessed some organizations try to pull it off without possessing the right motives, when most likely there was someone at the helm — a CEO, an owner, a chairman — who was not in agreement because he or she did not have a relationship with Christ. Without full commitment from the very top of the organization, any attempt in building a Kingdom Minded organization will be for naught. <u>Having a Christ follower at the helm is a given</u> and therefore not included as one of the seven premises listed below that we must accept and hold as truths in order to fully be capable of developing a Kingdom Minded organization:

1. Sharing Jesus in the Workplace
    Christian Leaders Must Be Modern Day Apostles

2. Aiming For the Best
    Be Diligent to Avoid Mediocrity

3. Abundant Life – In the Workplace
    Leave Sheaves Behind and Be Rewarded

4. Fearfully and Wonderfully Made Employees
    Using the Talents From Within Your Organization

5. Creating a Welcoming Workplace
    Creating an Environment of Excitement and Ease for Employees

6. Management Must Step Up
    Leading Your Employees into Success

7. Rewarding Your Hard Workers
    Good Standing Employees Deserve More Than Fair Wages

Let's first reflect on this passage as it often times is a guiding light for many Christian leaders. Colossians 3:17 "And whatever you do, whether in word or deed, do it all in the name of the Lord Jesus, giving thanks to God the Father through him."

Let's examine each premise in greater detail to help develop the foundation that is necessary in the start of building a Kingdom Minded organization.

1. Sharing Jesus in the Workplace

Jesus drew together the Apostles and taught them all they needed to know to return to their workplaces and evangelize. He equipped them with the necessary tools to complete the job. He then sent them out with the message, a message that would change the world.

In the past several months, as I have been blessed to have expanded my circle of friendship with an incredible assortment of people, I have been fortunate to have connected with pastors, church members, staff members and representatives across a broad spectrum of Christian churches. This exposure has afforded me the opportunity to gain a better understanding of the customs and norms of Mennonites, Amish, Charismatic, Baptist, Lutheran, Presbyterian, Ukrainian Baptist, Brethren, Assembly of God, Catholic, nondenominational and Evangelical churches. I really believe all of these church members believe in their core that the message of salvation is through the acceptance and agreement that Christ is the Lord of your life.

I am confident we can all agree on this essential tenet, but where, as a Christ follower, I perceive the complexity to be is to what degree does this love of God require us to share it with others? I would argue that you can't truly love God and contain the joy of this love. It will overflow out of you into the community and out to others, to the point where others will look at you and want to experience this joy, too.

The point is that when we truly love God, we must share the gospel with others; not to do so would abrogate our responsibility to God. I hope that you can agree with this, because it is an important foundation in setting the groundwork for building a Kingdom Minded organization.

Christian Leaders Must Be Modern Day Apostles

>*Deuteronomy 30*[8] *"You will again obey the LORD and follow all His commands I am giving you today.* [9] *Then the LORD your God will make you most prosperous in all the work of your hands and in the fruit of your womb, the young of your livestock and the crops of your land. The LORD will again delight in you and make you prosperous, just as He delighted in your ancestors,* [10] *if you obey the LORD your God and keep His commands and decrees that are written in this Book of the Law and turn to the LORD your God with all your heart and with all your soul."*

How long do we manage our organization without God before we realize that prosperity comes when we include Him? Having met with hundreds of Christian business professionals, I repeatedly run into a common thread: we go to church on Sunday and turn off our Christianity on Monday. How long must we all go on until we come to the realization that <u>Church is every day</u>?

Christian leaders are modern day apostles.

Christ ordained his apostles and *sent them back to work*. Their work included fishing, accounting and even tax collection. Christ did not demand that they stop working; they ministered in the marketplace. So, today, all of us who are Christian business and nonprofit leaders are <u>modern day apostles</u>. If your Christianity doesn't stop on Sunday night, if you build it into your leadership and your organization's values, you are building a Kingdom Minded organization.

2. AIMING FOR THE BEST

I don't think any organization can justify being mediocre. On the contrary, I believe that organizations have an obligation to their people to be excellent, to be world class, to be highly performing. Far too many organizations, ministries, churches, and nonprofits fall victim to a defeatist attitude.

I believe an organization should strive to become excellent, otherwise it should simply cease its existence before doing far greater harm than good. Too many people become discouraged by the slow deterioration of quality within organizations. People have become accustomed to allowing organizations to die a slow death rather than cutting them off at the right time and moving on. We should do it with excellence, or not do it at all.

Be Diligent and Avoid Mediocrity

Leviticus 25 [14] *"If you sell land to any of your own people or buy land from them, do not take advantage of each other.* [15] *You are to buy from your own people on the basis of the number of years since the Jubilee. And they are to sell to you on the basis of the number of years left for harvesting crops.* [16] *When the years are many, you are to increase the price, and when the years are few, you are to decrease the price, because what is really being sold to you is the number of crops."*

In today's competitive world, organizations are experiencing pricing pressures like never before. Being a second or third choice of customers will more than likely put you out of business. The knee-jerk reaction to cut corners, short customers, overcharge, or underbid a job with the intention of up-charging later is all too real.

Be diligent in your decision making. Be faithful and so shall He.

Every day, you and your employees are faced with making choices to do the right thing even when you believe it may ultimately harm your organization. But that, dear reader, is faulty thinking. When we put our trust in Christ and do the right thing, make the right choices and stay truthful in our business lives, we will outlive the others. If you are killing the mediocre monster, you are winning the battle.

Always ensure you hold the non-performers accountable!

One of the most difficult aspects of being a Christian business leader is disciplining those who are not pulling their weight. Many leaders prefer to ignore the behavior or order another direct report to intervene. Don't allow this to continue in your organization. Even God's word has something to say about it!

Proverbs 21:25: *"The craving of a sluggard will be the death of him, because his hands refuse to work."*

Be passionate and direct with your underperformers. You must manage those who are killing your organization. Be fair, but use discipline if necessary. Only in this way can you ensure that you are building the strong foundation of a Kingdom Minded organization.

3. Abundant Life – In the Workplace

It is often a subject of controversy as to whether prosperity is a good or bad thing in the eyes of God. We all see extremes: there are those in church leadership who go over the top in their views of financial prosperity. There are, however, other extremes — just consider monks and nuns. My personal view is that for most of us this place of prosperity lies somewhere in the middle. The first thing we must understand is that if you are reading this in the United States you are probably blessed with far greater prosperity than you realize.

Consider these common facts for a moment:

- If you have your own PC at home, you own something that costs more than the average person earns in an entire year in Somalia or Sierra Leone.

- If you have food in your fridge, clothes on your back, a roof over your head, and a place to sleep, you are richer than 75 percent of the world.

- If you have money in the bank, your wallet, and some spare change, you are among the top wealthiest eight percent in the world.

- If you woke up this morning with more health than illness, you are more blessed than the million people who will not survive this week.

- If you have never experienced the dangers of battle, the agony of imprisonment or torture, or the horrible pangs of starvation, you are luckier than 500 million people alive today.

- If you can read this message, you are more fortunate than three billion people in the world who are illiterate.

Bearing in mind such statistics, we must agree that we are materially successful already; we just don't realize how much. Success lies in the eye of the beholder and we possess varying definitions of what success is and should be. But let's consider prosperity for a moment. I define prosperity as the ability, after first giving to God via a tithe, to sustain a typical lifestyle that fits within your societal norm, with money left over to further the Kingdom and your family.

When reviewing scripture, I have concluded that God promises us through the Law of Divine Return in Luke 6:38: "Give, and it will be given to you. A good measure, pressed down, shaken together and running over, will be poured into your lap. For with the measure you use, it will be measured to you." When we give back through tithing and advancing His Kingdom, it returns to us. However, I don't do it for the return. I do it for God, and I believe it will, and I have witnessed it, come back!

I also see through scripture that God promises happiness, health, benefits and peace in Psalm 35:27: "May those who delight in my vindication shout for joy and gladness; may they always say, 'The LORD be exalted, who delights in the well-being of His servant.'" He further promises that we will be prospered in order to bless in Deuteronomy 8:18: "But remember the LORD your God, for it is He who gives you the ability to produce wealth, and so confirms His covenant, which He swore to your ancestors, as it is today."

The New Testament shares this with us: Hebrews 13:16 "And do not forget to do good and to share with others, for with such sacrifices God is pleased. "

And, finally, it is clear that God has promised us an abundant life in John 10:10: "The thief comes only to steal and kill and destroy; I have come that they may have life, and have it to the full." God promises that if we do everything He asks we will prosper. Philippians 4:19: "And my God will meet all your needs according to the riches of His glory in Christ Jesus."

God's word says that if we do what He asks, prosperity is assured. I believe this, but it doesn't matter what I believe. Do you?

Leave Sheaves Behind and Be Rewarded

> **Deuteronomy 24:19:** *"When you are harvesting in your field and you overlook a sheaf, do not go back to get it. Leave it for the foreigner, the fatherless and the widow, so that the LORD your God may bless you in all the work of your hands."*

When we live our lives in a compassionate and giving way, God has a way of replenishing our supply of resources. Oftentimes you will find that the more you give away the more you gain. It may sound absurd but I have experienced and witnessed it several times, not only in personal lives, but in many careers as well.

This is very important in the workplace. The more you coach and mentor your employees, the greater the reward they will reap, and you as well. Don't be selfish with your time. I have unfortunately met selfish leaders who never connected with their direct reports; this has grave consequences within the organization at the employee level.

Allow Your Employees to Enjoy the Organization's Harvest!

Connect with your people daily, share objectives with them, and create excitement within your team. Excited and passionate teams reap results. Most of all, leave sheaves behind for them. Be generous with your employees and let them enjoy the fruits of the organization's harvest. When you do this, you are building a Kingdom Minded organization that honors Christ.

4. Fearfully and Wonderfully Made Employees

I have coached hundreds of job seekers over the past several years. One common theme I encounter is the complaint that people's talents and strengths were never appreciated by their employers. This is unfortunate, but it is an absolute reality. In coaching leaders by utilizing the Myers Briggs Type Indicator (MBTI), I typically find that their personality traits hold little or no value for the contributions of others who are not "like" them. This is a great tragedy in the workplace.

When an organization is filled with diverse talent and a broad spectrum of strengths that are not being utilized, it's to the detriment of the organization and the leadership. Find out your employees' talents and unique gifts! Think of the overflowing potential right at your fingertips. We all have something to offer an organization. Until your personal leadership and your leaders around you realize it, you will be stifled.

In high-performing organizations people play to their strengths, Strengths are those things that give you energy, that get you going, and that make you want to do more. Marcus Buckingham preaches strengths and had a profound impact on me personally. Having used his video, "The Truth About You," in many of my leadership development courses, I finally "got it" the thirtieth time I watched it: "Mark, you are not good at grammar; you lose all your energy over it, but you are quite creative. So, focus on writing creatively and hire yourself a proofreader!" Amen, Marcus Buckingham, you hit a home run with me.

Use Your Talents from within Your Organization

Exodus 35:35 "He has filled them with skill to do all kinds of work as engravers, designers, embroiderers in blue, purple and scarlet yarn and fine linen, and weavers — all of them skilled workers and designers."

Most organizations are packed to the hilt with talented people! Oftentimes, the talents of the people are far greater than imagined because leaders have never tapped fully into them or attempted to discover what lies beneath. I once worked with an organization that spent thousands of dollars outsourcing the building of their website to a web design organization when it could have been built by one of their own employees. They had never taken the time to find out whether their own people possessed the resources, the vision, and the talent to do so. The organization chose to look elsewhere, when instead what they needed was right under their noses.

Don't spend thousands paying for something you already have!

Have you invested the time to identify your employees' hidden talents? The talents above and beyond their daily job requirements? Knowing the talents of the people working for you and drawing on them regularly will ignite your workplace! You will be building a Kingdom Minded organization and inspiring your employees.

5. A Welcoming Workplace

This is perhaps the premise that gets me the most animated, having witnessed some of the worst work environments imaginable. Unfortunately, these workplaces were not in third world countries — these were right here in the United States! One organization had people cooking and eating in a filthy, oil-ridden machine shop. I witnessed employees having to use urine containers because their supervisors refused to provide the proper relief to employees on promised intervals. One of the worst situations was watching an executive pull into the parking lot with a brand new luxury car just after announcing plant closures and salary reductions. I call that unquestionably insensitive and arrogant, family money or not.

You can tell a lot about an organization within the first few minutes of a visit. I have made several sales calls in the past when, as soon as I entered the lobby, I had to will myself to keep from turning and running out the door. What kept me from making my escape was the realization that they needed my help the most to see the error of their ways. Conversely, I have worked with organizations in some of the grimiest industries imaginable that had the cleanest facilities for their beloved, content employees.

The litmus test is somewhat easy and resonates with leaders. I ask them whether they would want their daughter to work at their organization in the middle of the manufacturing environment, to use the rest rooms designated for employees, or eat in the organization's break rooms. If they say yes then their organization is likely being managed correctly. If they say no then something is very wrong. If they are not up to speed for the leader's daughter, then they are not up to speed for anyone else, and certainly not for one's precious employees.

There are other characteristics that cause organizations to be terrible places. This includes but is not limited to: a lack of resources, mismanagement or complete lack of management, unnecessarily onerous work schedules as a result of bad planning, lack of engagement, lack of direction — the list goes on.

Create an Environment of Excitement and Ease For Employees

> **Genesis 2:15** *"The LORD God took the man and put him in the Garden of Eden to work it and take care of it."*

From the very beginning of time, we have been blessed with work. Work is an inevitable part of our lives. When we are not working, we are thinking about work. Work preoccupies us. Work defines us, feeds us, and prospers us. Work is the foundation of our society and our world. Work, my friends, is not going away. If work is inevitable, why must it be so miserable at so many workplaces?

If work is inevitable, why allow it to be bad?

If we are honest with ourselves, we know the reason: it is leadership, plain and simple. Any workplace that employees perceive as bad will always point back to a lack of competent leadership. I am not saying that work should be a utopian environment! There will always be elements of discomfort because of its nature, which includes the pressures of responsibility for a job well done. It's not fishing or a day at the beach! Leaders: make sure work is a good place for your employees. Employees should be at ease coming to work because they know they have managers who care, and they should be excited to be part of your organization. Work can be enjoyable and meaningful for those you employ.

If you manage your business with the kind of leadership that creates a culture of inclusion, prosperity, and a shared vision, while fostering family love and relationships, then you are to be lauded: you are building a Kingdom Minded organization.

6. Management Must Step Up

One of the greatest organizational challenges we face as a country is our lack of leadership talent. Leadership is not developed in young people like it was many years ago. In days gone by, our youth were encouraged to gain leadership experiences in Girl and Boy Scouting, where they learned to lead others effectively. There is a vast difference between managing and leading. Anyone can manage. I can appoint a manager who can go out and manage the next day. Leading is a totally different concept, a concept many people all too often confuse with managing. Leading involves creating buy-in and influence versus managers who are more cause and effect or carrot and stick-oriented.

Not only have we missed out with developing our future generations to be leaders, but we have a whole generation of young people who have been taught that everyone gets a prize irrespective of merit, that leadership is everyone's responsibility, and that all should share in the success and all should be self-led. Couple this with corporations eliminating training and development departments and any budgeting for leadership development, either internal or external to the organization, and we are left with a gaping void in available leadership.

Often, as I begin training an organization in basic leadership skills, such as communication or "Servant Leadership," I discover that it is the first time any of the leaders in the room have ever attended any formal session on leadership. I find it both shocking and dismaying; we are being led by people who were promoted to a leadership role simply because they were good at their previous jobs. Hence, organizations are being run by really good widget makers, not skilled leaders.

In one situation, an employee rose through the organization through a litany of errors and missteps by owners and board members to the position of CEO, despite never having led more than four or five people at a time, and those were in a technical function, not an environment of cross-departmental responsibilities. Inevitably, the CEO fails miserably. In this particular case, the organization struggles to this day from his lack of leadership skills.

In order for an organization to prosper and function as a Kingdom Minded organization, it must possess appropriate and capable leadership talent. If you are managing an organization and ever wonder whether you have the right leadership to navigate your organization correctly, then you probably don't. Seek good and wise counsel. Contact a trustworthy leadership consulting group and have them spend some time accessing your leadership team's capabilities. You will be glad you did.

Leading Your Employees into Success

Nehemiah 6:9 *"They were all trying to frighten us, thinking, 'Their hands will get too weak for the work, and it will not be completed.'"*

Have you heard leaders exclaim that the workers of today are just plain lazy? That they are not motivated and have no idea how to put in a day's work? It is a common complaint, heard over and over. Some training firms even offer seminars on the topic! It cannot be said, however, that all workers operate in this way. We live in a society devoid of leadership capable of and willing to lead employees to excellence. Rather than turning the work culture into a negative one, we should ask ourselves whether we are developing a high-performing organization.

In high-performing, Christ-honoring organizations, leaders lead and dream big. They have a *Vision, a Mission, and strong Values* in place for their organizations. When you have these in place and properly integrated, you:

- memorialize your standards;
- provide guiding principles in all you do;
- make your values easily understood by employees; and
- drive a value-based culture with your customers.

So, ask yourself: Do we have a shared vision with our organization's people? Are we communicating that vision of what our organization wants to become? Are we creating a culture of inclusion, of truly being a team? Or are we an organization segregated into workers and higher-ups? If you are following these principles, you are building a Kingdom Minded organization.

7. Rewarding Your Hard Workers

We have it wrong. We often blame the condition of the organization on its people when, in fact, it is usually not the people with the problem: it is the leadership not demonstrating leadership skills that is the problem. Lack of leadership will hurt an organization; worse, it will ultimately kill your morale.

I believe 99.9 percent of employees in any given organization want to do well. They want to exceed set goals, they want to go home feeling satisfied that they have contributed to their organization's success, and to know they've made a positive difference. Unfortunately, employees often lack leaders who can or are willing to help them self-actualize to reach this realm of possibility.

This past summer I found myself sitting in a coffee shop observing a manager who spent all of his time texting on his cell phone when he was supposed to be supervising his staff. It is this type of self-absorbed leadership behavior that hurts organizations. I have a better leadership approach: coach your managers, set goals for them, detail your customer service expectations, *and lead by example*. (I was fully expecting to see this manager criticize a subordinate for texting but was relieved that I did not witness that behavior.)

Employees with well thought out job descriptions, including their input, shared goals and objectives, proper amounts of feedback, and coaching, will benefit and prosper their organization. Without these, employees kill their organizations, not because they want to, not because they are deliberately doing so, but because it is the simple byproduct of not being led. When they're not led properly, employees become complacent, unengaged, and ineffective. Behind every bad restaurant experience, every missed shipment date, every lost package, and every bad service call is bad leadership. Don't always assume it is solely the fault of one bad employee.

Good-Standing Employees Deserve More Than Fair Wages

1 Timothy 5:18 *"For Scripture says, 'Do not muzzle an ox while it is treading out the grain,' and 'The worker deserves his wages.'"*

Wow! The ox was permitted to eat during its workday. Sadly, many organizations don't extend the same consideration to the most valuable commodity of their business — their employees! Many years ago I witnessed a young teen working at a local pizza shop making minimum wage. The owner was a cruel, selfish man who refused to provide any food or beverage to his employees unless purchased at full price. The owner's children would come in and help themselves to all kinds of food that they left half-eaten, to be thrown away, but the floor sweepers got nothing. The shop owner also insisted upon destroying any leftover items at the end of each evening rather than offering to share them with his employees. Dear Christian business leaders please do not fall victim to becoming a tyrant in your workplace. Be generous when you can. It is an investment that pays huge dividends in the Body of Christ and in your business.

Be generous to your people and you shall be rewarded!

Some of the most impactful gestures of gratitude and appreciation that I have given my people were the least costly — small lunch celebrations or boxes of favorite chocolates. If you act with kind regard, with generous giving, you are building a strong Kingdom Minded organization while honoring Christ.

Remember: virtually every single employee will give you 100 percent when they know you care!

Lastly in relation to this premise, it is important to reflect on this piece of scripture. 1 Timothy 6:17-19 [17] "Command those who are rich in this present world not to be arrogant nor to put their hope in wealth, which is so uncertain, but to put their hope in God, who richly provides us with everything for our enjoyment. [18] Command them to do good, to be rich in good deeds, and to be generous and willing to share. [19] In this way they will lay up treasure for themselves as a firm foundation for the coming age, so that they may take hold of the life that is truly life." Because in the end we really are left with nothing to take with us. So why are we hesitant to share with the people who we should care about the most?

PART THREE

1. What Is a Mission?

All successful organizations have a *Mission*. Without a Mission, no one will know what it is they are doing and why. Another problem organizations have when they're lacking a Mission is that their customers and vendors often end up confused and with mixed expectations.

I have worked for many organizations in my time. Probably more than most, and I consider this to be a good thing. The reason I consider this a good thing is that the experiences that God has given me in these numerous and diverse organizations has made me a far more competent counselor to businesses across the marketplace than if I had occupied one narrow niche for most of my career.

One common denominator I have identified is that the businesses that are successful all have an established Mission for their organization, a Mission that is <u>co-developed by all of their employees</u> and is ingrained into the culture of the organization. In fact, in high-performing organizations, candidates are exposed to the organization's Mission before they're even hired. Vendors know the Mission and customers are aware, as well.

When vendors know the Mission and customers understand it, that's enormously positive, but the most powerful and impactful group are your employees. In my wealth of experience, I have discovered an absolute truth by simply listening to employees for more than 20 years. Fully <u>99 percent of all employees who come to work every day, want nothing more than to do a good job</u>; in fact, most want to exceed your expectations. It really is the American way. Work hard, play hard and love your life. The problem is that many organizations suffer from is a lack of leadership to help steer the organization.

Specifically, they lack leadership in creating a Mission that employees own and strive to achieve.

What is a Mission?

Your *Mission* is simply what you do best — every day — and why. Your Mission should reflect your customers' needs. Having a Mission is the foundation of turning the dreams and potential of an organization into reality. In a nutshell, your Mission simply affirms why your organization exists!

So what does a Mission consist of? Well, it really is not rocket science. It is simply what your organization collectively — yes, I said collectively — not top down management, or board of directors to management — developed. It works like this:

1. The senior management team develops a framework of what they believe the Mission is and should be.
2. Line management then takes the draft document to the line supervision.
3. Finally, employees and a good HR rep facilitate a roundtable session using the draft Mission as a guide.

You have a couple of reiterations, meetings back and forth, and then it's time for "Congratulations!" because you now have a consensus on your Mission. Remember that when the Mission is being facilitated, the facilitator must be skilled in getting everyone on board with the final product.

Key is letting your employees know that each one of them has an opportunity to challenge it, provide their personal input and suggest changes, but ultimately, when the majority of the employees and management agree to the final document, then it is up to all employees to respect and support it.

Benefits of Creating or Revisiting Your Mission

The benefit of creating a Mission or revisiting a current one is that it opens up the communication process inside of your organization. An effective Mission is based on input and commitment from as many people within your organization as possible. A Mission statement should not be an autocratic version of Moses and the Tablets. All of your employees must feel and understand your organization's Mission. Only then can they make the necessary personal commitment to its spirit.

Tips for great Mission Statements:

- Keep it short.
- Describe WHY customers will buy from you.
- Define your product or service clearly.
- Identify WHO is your ideal customer.
- Specify WHAT you offer your customer — benefits, services, advantages, etc.
- Delineate what makes your product or service different from that of your competition.

Examples:

Google: "We organize the world's information and make it universally accessible and useful."

Starbucks: "We inspire and nurture the human spirit — one person, one cup, and one neighborhood at a time."

2. Organizational Vision

High-performing organizations have a clearly defined *Vision*. The *Vision* helps guide all its employees and supervision to their desired destination and explains why. Organizations with a *Vision* have a workplace of direction, purpose, and achievement. Vision-driven organizations know where they want to be, and do the appropriate things to get there. All along the way, they have employees who enthusiastically support the *Vision.*

What Is an Organizational Vision?

The best *Vision* is one that has been created, or at least contributed to, by all employees of the organization. Like the *Mission*, the more buy-in the organization has, the greater the effectiveness of the Vision. The Vision should be inspiring! It is where you want to be. The Vision is what's occurring as you deliver on your Mission.

It is where you want your organization to be in five years. We define it as five years but you may prefer to extend that, or, if you are a start-up, you may want to start with a three-year Vision. We prefer five years because that is a reasonable amount of time for most organizations to get to the next step. The Vision must be realistically achievable. If you own a pizza shop, it would not be wise to say your Vision is to grow to a $2 billion-dollar market value. Instead, an achievable Vision might look like: "We will grow to be a regional choice by consumers by expanding to 10 locations."

Reflect on the following questions for building your *Vision*:

1. How are the market and customer base changing in the next three to seven years?
2. How will that create opportunities for the organization?
3. How can we meet the gap between now and our Vision?
4. How will we surpass our competitors and seek greater market share?
5. What are we doing collectively to capitalize on the changes in business conditions and needs of the business?

Examples:

Amazon "Our vision is to be earth's most customer-centric organization; to build a place where people can come to find and discover anything they might want to buy online."

Nike "To be the number one athletic company in the world."

What is the difference between Mission and Vision?

The most asked question to us surrounding *Mission, Vision and Core Values* is: what is the difference between a Mission and a Vision? <u>Your Mission is what you do best every day. Your Vision is what the future looks like when you deliver on your Mission exceedingly well.</u>

High-performing Organizations

There is, unquestionably, a key to high-performing organizations. That key is Vision — a Vision that ignites employees to achieve great things!

When I worked with the Gatorade™ Division of Quaker Oats™, we smoked the competition. Why? We had Vision. And every employee working there bought into that Vision. Powerade™ and All Sport™ didn't have a chance. In fact, where is All Sport today? If Gatorade did not take them out completely, they certainly limited their capabilities.

The problem is not with workers in the U.S. What we have today is a problem with leadership — leadership that lacks the ability to create buy-in for excellence in Vision achievement.

If you are a leader you must develop a Vision, and develop it with employee input. If you are an employee, make sure you buy into your organization's Vision. If it needs tweaking, ask to do so with respect. Your leadership will appreciate your interest!

3. ORGANIZATIONAL CORE VALUES

Organizations tend to be meshed together by a unique blend of personal and corporate values. These values are important to its employees, leaders, and stakeholders.

What exactly is a *Core Value*? From our human resources perspective, a Core Value reflects the heart of your organization. It is what makes your organization tick; it defines your organization. It is how your vendors view your behavior toward them; it is your culture when dealing with customers.

It is what employees tell their neighbors and friends when they ask what it is like to work at your organization.

One of the most important aspects of Core Values is where they come from. Core Values need to be shared across the organization, but they also need to have a reference point. Your Core Values should include a statement highlighting that reference point.

Example:

We are a family-owned and operated organization. We respect each other and collectively support the following values in our business.

Efficiency: We pride ourselves on speed — and, yes, we are accurate!

Individual Responsibility: We believe in holding ourselves accountable. We deliver on our own promises and we always endeavor to use good judgment.

Quality: We do not compromise on quality. Quality is job one.

Ownership: We own our decisions, we own our mistakes, and we own our achievements.

If you have not yet defined what your Core Values are, now is the best time. Solidify an agreement on which Core Values are important to your organization. This should be done with care because leaders and employees often create their own values; they are not always aligned with the owners' or senior managers' Core Values.

In the development of Core Values for a seasoned organization, the process should be shared, not just top down. Brainstorming should include several layers of employees and are often best done in focus group format, where groups of employees nominate a representative to meet with the facilitator. The ensuing Core Values should be agreed upon and understood by all employees.

Naturally, there are some Core Values that are nonnegotiable, such as trust or integrity. However, the true heart of the organization is what is valued collectively by employees, and is not necessarily always what the top leaders think or want.

How many Core Values do you need?

Some organizations have as many as ten Core Values. We believe that is too many. Instead, we recommend three to five Core Values. Fewer Core Values not only ensures that these are your true core principles but also makes it easier for your employees to remember them easily. It is also easier to manage within your HR processes.

Below is a laundry list of the Core Values that we find most valuable. This list will enable you to best select what is truly most important to your organization.

Accountability — We are responsible for our actions, which, in turn, influence our customers, vendors and coworkers. We hold ourselves and each other to a high standard of accountability.

Balance — We create a work environment that promotes healthy lifestyles and celebrates family-work balance for employees.

Biblical Principles — We are a organization founded on Biblical principles, therefore, all we do we entrust to God.

Civic Responsibility — We honor our coworkers and our communities by our motivation, knowledge, and ability to actively participate in our communities as volunteers and leaders.

Compassion — We show kindness for others by helping those who are in need.

Courage — We face difficult situations with confidence and determination and stand up for our convictions, even when some of the decisions we make are right, but not popular.

Commitment — We are committed to ourselves, our vendors, and our customers; it is through commitment that we will all achieve.

Community — We are committed to the communities in which we do business and our employees live, work, and love.

Consistency — We pride ourselves on our reputation for consistency.

Diversity — We respect diversity of race, gender, thought, interests, and ideas.

Efficiency — We pride ourselves on speed — and, yes, we are accurate!

Empowerment — We create an atmosphere that allows others to achieve through their unique contributions.

Fairness — We pride ourselves on having a work environment that emulates fairness. We treat people equally and make decisions without influence from favoritism or prejudice.

Fun — Work does not need to be painful or joyless.

Honesty — We believe in consistently seeking and speaking the truth in the workplace. We believe in a workplace devoid of lying, cheating, stealing, or any other forms of deception.

Individual Responsibility — We believe in holding ourselves accountable. We deliver on our own promises, and we always use good judgment.

Industriousness — We realize the intrinsic and extrinsic rewards of putting forth efforts to achieve our goals; we celebrate our team's unique abilities to contribute to prospering our organization.

Innovation — We create before others do!

Integrity — Without integrity, we are nothing!

Justice — We consider the perspectives of others and demonstrate the courage to be consistently fair while treating all with equal dignity and respect.

Leadership — We lead with conviction and understanding.

Ownership — We own our decisions; we own our mistakes; we own our achievements.

Passion — We love what we do, and our heart goes into our work.

Quality — We do not compromise on quality. Quality is job one.

Respect — We maintain a work style of trust in all our interactions.

Respect — We value our vendors, our customers and ourselves; we treat others as we would want ourselves to be treated.

Risk Taking — We take calculated risks, learn from our mistakes, and grow in our successes.

Safety — We are accountable for our personal safety and helping our coworkers maintain a safe environment.

Service Excellence — We provide best in class service to our internal and external customers every day.

The best Core Value is one that you and your teams identify and create together.

Part Four: Integration

After the Mission, Vision, and Values

Most leaders, after they finalize the recreation of their *Mission, Vision, and Values* (MVV) for their organizations, do what comes naturally — they share it with everyone. It then goes up on the organization's website and it gets printed poster-sized and hung on conference rooms walls and in the lobby. It's mentioned consistently for about three months … and then it dies.

It dies because it is not an intrinsic part of the way you do business. It is not ingrained into the soul of your organization.

How do you make your *Mission, Vision, and Values* a part of the way in which you do business? <u>You integrate it into the practices that are always connected to the people that make it happen</u> — you integrate it into the people who are applying your HR practices. HR practices are practices that touch all employees.

What are some examples of HR practices?
- Employee Relations
- Recruitment Management
- Workforce Planning
- On Boarding Management
- Training Management
- Performance Management

- Compensation & Benefits
- Attendance and Leave Management
- Compensation and Benefits Management
- Employee Development Skill Management
- Health & Safety
- Employee Activities
- Employment Policy Management

You could probably laundry-list 40-plus practices, but for the sake of explanation, we are going to provide guidance on six key practices that you can integrate with your MVV quite easily (see Appendix). These six are your:

1. Handbook
2. Recruitment Process
3. Performance Review Process
4. Job Descriptions
5. Communication Process
6. Training and Development

Over the next few chapters, we will walk you through the integration of the MVV into each one of these practices. Think about what your experience has been when integrating these concepts into your organization's practices.

Don't just hang your *Vision, Mission, and Core Values* on the wall! Integrate, integrate and then integrate some more. Get your values into your work culture and make it an intrinsic part of the way you work.

1. Integrate — Making Employee Handbooks Reflect Your Culture

Employees complain when you don't have a handbook, but when you have one they often don't want it! An employee handbook is very easy to create, but probably the most overlooked aspect of employment documentation. One thing is for sure: if an organization has multiple shifts or multiple locations or just multiple employees, an employee handbook can certainly help keep all employees on the same page. Handbooks are always a delicate subject.

When done right and with employee input, this tool can make a positive difference.

- Make it reflect your *Mission, Vision, and Values* (MVV)
- Make it relevant
- Keep it simple
- Keep it legal and legit

Reflect your MVV

Your handbook should be an absolute reflection of your MVV, which essentially amplifies your culture. Someone who is unfamiliar with your organization should be able to pick up your handbook and see your organization's heart simply by the tone and the guiding principles you lay out for your employees. The front of the handbook should contain your MVV, followed by the President's message as to why the MVV is important to the organization and how it was created.

Make it Relevant

Having reviewed hundreds of handbooks over the years, I can say that most are useless. They are irrelevant, often don't convey the culture of the organization, and are more about preaching or dictating than guiding.

Keep it Simple

A handbook should not contain every scrap of information about the organization. Worse yet, it should not contain every possible scenario in which an employee violation could occur. Keep it simple and you will have a greater impact than if you over-complicate or over-stimulate the reader. Many employees I've spoken with over the years tell me that if a handbook is interesting they will read it to learn more about the organization. However, if it rambles on over policy and procedures, most will put it down after two pages. The ideal handbook will inspire the reader to learn more about the organization.

Keep it Legal and Legit

Always ensure you include the appropriate legal clauses. There are far too many to list here but a few that come to mind speak to ADA, FMLA, Employment at Will, EEOC etc. You want to make sure you cover your bases.

Think about your experiences with employee handbooks.

How did the ones that you have used fit your organization? Did they match your culture? Did they drive the behaviors the organization and employees desire?

In closing, it is important to note that having a handbook is oftentimes the only opportunity for employers to memorialize what is expected of employees. But always include what employees can expect of you! A handbook should never be a one way street of core policies of the organization; if it is, you will chill the warmth right out of the organization. Set a positive, inspiring tone in the handbook.

2. Integrate — Developing World Class Recruitment Strategies

Perhaps one of the most difficult aspects of managing organizations is the act of recruitment. It is not necessarily difficult only on the candidates; it's also difficult on organizations as well. Even though we are living in tumultuous business times, with real unemployment exceeding 10 percent in almost every city in our nation, recruitment is still a challenge for a variety of reasons, including but not limited to:

- Lack of skilled candidates
- Wounded and hurt applicants lacking trust of any organization
- Having too many candidates to choose from makes it difficult to know where to begin
- Salary expectation alignment; many candidates are accustomed to more

These are all hurdles to climb over in the hiring process. However, organizations that have a well thought out process and strategy will prevail in hiring the best candidates to accelerate the performance of the organization. The entire process of building a "Kingdom Minded" organization revolves around including your MVV into every HR practice as practicable. The recruitment process is not excluded.

In developing your strategy, you should weave into the process several concepts that will help recruit the best candidates within your Mission, reach your Vision, and operate within your Values. Your process should include:

1. Networking your vacancies to trusted sources
2. Using employee referral systems to increase your candidate pool

3. Use consistent hiring methodology when recruiting candidates

4. Always include your MVV in the recruitment process

Networking

Most organizations, because of turnover within their HR department, or a lack of HR professionals within the organization, do not have a formalized network to which they can announce vacancies. This is a concerning drawback to the process. Organizations should consistently mine for talent and the community should be aware of the organization and have a general idea of what they do and what their hiring patterns are. Organizations should spend time marketing themselves as a great place to work; this is also an effective form of marketing to potential customers. People want to buy products and services from organizations that treat their employees well. Start networking with churches, Christian colleges, LinkedIn groups, alumni associations, nonprofit executives, mission organizations, seminaries — the list goes on. The problem is that many organizations do not create such a network list. Network today; it will pay dividends in years to come.

Employee Referral Systems

Nine out of ten organizations I meet with do not have either a formal or informal employee referral systems for candidates. If they do have one, it is stale and not yielding any results. This is unfortunate, because people want to work with people who match the organization culture, and knowhow and want to get the job done. Reinvent this program or develop it if you don't have one. The easiest way to do so is to bring together a cross section of employees for half an hour and ask: would you refer your friends to work here? If not, why not? And what do we need to do to make this an environment that you would want to refer them to? Delve into what the referral reward should be in the program. Some miserly HR folks suggest one to two hundred-dollar bonuses. Considering a Monster board ad is three hundred dollars, not to mention the hassle of screening 10 to 20 candidates to get to one good candidate, don't you think this is a bit stingy? Reward your people!

Consistent Hiring Methodology

Lack of a consistent hiring methodology will get you burned. Getting an EEOC or Human Relations commission charge becomes not an "if" proposition but a "when." Stepping outside of the legal concerns, why not take the high road right off and ensure your practice is beyond reproach? When recruiting, always have a job description, always have interview evaluation sheets, and always have decent but not copious notes of the candidate selection meeting when all interviewers give input. I have experienced some embarrassing situations at all levels of the organization where a document to support hiring or not hiring candidates didn't even exist. If you don't have this in place, make sure you keep your checkbook handy. You will need it.

And finally, include your MVV in your recruitment process. When candidates see this, they are intrigued, especially when the presenter presents it in a way that is exciting.

Candidates love to see prospective employers who truly believe in the Mission, Vision, and Values of their organization.

Organizations have lost their mojo. Show candidates your passion! Most people want to work for a organization that has direction. They are tired of the lack of leadership in government, in corporate America, and their local schools. The last thing they want to do is join a organization that is weak and non-directional. Show them your passion through your MVV!

Explain to each candidate your *Mission, Vision, and Values,* where they came from, and why you have them. Let them know that you are an organization founded on Christian principles. Most often the reaction I get from candidates when they hear this is, "Wow! Finally a place that might treat me with dignity and respect."

Don't worry about offending anyone. You are not pushing your values onto them; you are simply demonstrating what they are. I have had candidates say that they are not Christians, but that working for a organization like ours would help them understand Christianity better. Exposing people to Christ — that is what we all desire. That is the work God really wants us to focus on.

Reflect on your experiences in recruitment. Are there any best practices you have used but are not using them now? <u>Be a difference maker today</u>. Improve your recruitment process and help your organization today and into the future.

3. Integrate — Job Descriptions Make a Difference

For many years I witnessed leadership at a variety of levels in several organizations struggle to see the value of certain HR practices. One practice of uncertain value within HR that always seems to pop up is job descriptions.

Why do you need job descriptions? Do organizations really use them? We created some 5 years ago; will they work? Are they just an old school personnel requirement? Well, you actually need them for a variety of reasons, such as to:

- Reiterate your *Mission, Vision and Values* (MVVs)
- Align employees with shared goals
- Use as an effective hiring tool
- Reinforce what is required from your employees and why

Reiteration of your Mission, Vision, and Values

Job descriptions should remind employees what the overall objective is for their position. Why? Because that objective should tie in to whatever the Mission and Vision of the organization are. Without a clear objective statement, both new and current employees won't understand why it is they do what they are asked to do. That might sound a little crazy, but I have met hundreds of employees over the years who, when asked why they do what they do at work, they had no answer. When employees know the objective and why they exist in their roles, they are self-driven to exceed that objective.

We are not becoming lazy as a nation; we are becoming unguided!

It is the greatest fallacy of the workplace that we have become merely lazy, when in fact, it stems mostly from lack of leadership and experience in guiding employees to excellence.

Align Employees

Employees should be involved in the development of their job descriptions. They should gain ownership in the process and fully understand how their position relates to others within the organization and how each position depends on the other for performance. HR can champion the process and keep track of the descriptions themselves.

The creation of the description should be done by the employee and employee's manager.

One of the best-run organizations I have had the pleasure to work with linked all the descriptions for each of their positions on a shared Local Area Network while also visually linking all employees together via an electronic organizational chart. It left no one wondering who was responsible for doing what, while reporting to whom, and why.

A Hiring Tool

A candidate should never be interviewed without a formal job description in hand. There is no way to assess a candidate fairly without this basic tool. High-performing organizations have recruitment processes that included the revision of the job description while, at the same time, the development of relevant questions for the interview process itself. Want to inspire interest in a candidate? Give them the job description, because almost no organizations do this. When people know what it is they are required to do, it creates interest and potential ownership once they are hired.

Reinforce What is Required and Why

Repetition is a good thing. When job descriptions repeat important information that is reflected in other areas of the organization, it reinforces the importance of that information.

When employees see the same messages over and over from a variety of sources and tied to several processes, it means something to them. It leaves an imprint.

This is why building in language that reiterates the commitment to living up to your organization's Mission and striving for your Vision will help get your employees going in the right direction collectively. It is also important to capture the expected behaviors in the job description, as they relate to the Values of your organization.

Essential to all job descriptions are: the purpose of the position, position requirements (education and or experience), and physical requirements/environmental conditions. Of course you should always include the statement: "This description is not designed to cover or contain a comprehensive listing of activities, duties or responsibilities required of an incumbent. An incumbent may be asked to perform other duties as required." This statement ensures that you don't have folks walking around saying, "That's not in my job description!"

Reflect on your experiences with job descriptions; what good and bad experiences have you had in dealing with job descriptions? Are they a waste of time from your perspective or have you witnessed employees flourish when using them?

4. Integrate — Successful Performance Reviews

Probably one of the least liked HR processes of all organizations is the dreaded performance review. However, it does not have to be that way. Performance reviews should be beneficial not only to the organization but to the employee. Key components to a successful process include:

- Built-in commitment to your MVV
- Shared goals and objectives throughout the organization
- Employee ownership of career and job performance
- Simplistic but meaningful processes
- Solid guidelines and commitment from senior leadership

Commitment to Your MVV

If you want your team to fulfill your organization's Mission, reach your Vision, and operate within your Values, you must build these into the performance review process. When you do, it shows the organization that leadership believes in the MVV so much that they have included it in the measurement of employment performance. Ensure your goals and objectives are aligned with your Mission and Vision; if they are not, you must question why they are in place. Most organizations that we support appreciate us walking them through a simple Strengths, Weaknesses, Opportunities, and

Threats (SWOT) analysis to help develop goals for the organization. In the area of Values, always build your values and other important values into the behavior section of the performance review form; we will discuss behaviors in more detail later in this chapter.

Shared Goals and Objectives

In high performing organizations, including those that I have worked for, have all had performance review processes that were aligned to shared goals and objectives through the organization. Typically the scenario worked like this: The CEO would develop four to six goals and objectives that would then be approved or renegotiated by the board of directors. Those goals would cascade through the organization all the way down to, for example, the third-shift sanitation employee at the plant in Arkansas. The employees would align what they need to accomplish within their scope of authority against the goals of the person(s) above them.

The review process primarily focuses on annual goals and very little on the mundane aspects of day to day work reflective of what the job description dictates. The daily work should be accomplished, and if not, the employee should be managed through disciplinary procedures.

Employee Ownership

I have had the experience of employees approaching me earlier in my career at the end of the performance review cycle. Often their approach was because they never had met with their managers even one time during the course of the performance cycle.

Make no mistake: they are at fault as much as their inept management.

Employees must take ownership of their careers, their development, and their performance. Those who do not simply will not survive in this economy. Part of ensuring that they take ownership is ensuring that the process is clearly defined; the employee is obliged to prepare performance form materials and be proactive in scheduling a performance review meeting with their manager if the manager is not. If the manager still fails to meet with them, the employee has an obligation to go to HR or, absent HR, the manager's superior. Doing nothing should never be an option.

Simplistic but Meaningful Processes

Twelve-page forms and manuals that exceed sixty pages will just not work. Ensure your process includes easily understood documentation and a review form that does not exceed a good resume length. Two pages is enough. Keep the form limited to four to six operational goals and three to five behavior-based goals.

Never have a process that is void of behavioral objectives.

I have worked with several teams that insisted upon only production-related goals. They killed each other in the process to achieve them and when challenged, they would always say that they were not being measured on niceness, but solely on how many widgets they made! Balance your performance scorecard, and you will have better results.

Solid Guidelines and Commitment from Senior Leadership

When we describe "solid" guidelines, we mean guidelines that are not created in a vacuum, by one person high on a mountaintop. Guidelines should be developed by a cross-functional group of employees from a variety of areas within the organization. This brings a rich blend of thoughts and experiences to the table.

Most of the HR people that I worked with during my career were not capable of coming up with such solid guidelines without assistance.

It is a sad statement to make regarding my profession, but I gave up defending much of the deficiencies I discovered years ago.

Senior leadership must buy into the process and support it. If they don't, it is doomed to certain failure.

Years ago, I worked for an organization in which no matter how hard the CEO worked on convincing the president of a particular division to manage the performance review process, this president would balk. The division president's lack of commitment transcended the organization. The process became a joke and no one nurtured it. I look back at the organization now and wonder if things could have turned out differently. They have closed half of their plants and shed several thousand employees. Is it a stretch to link lay-offs to lack of leadership in embracing a performance review process? Perhaps not. I do believe that if innovation was a top goal heading into the downturn, that organization could conceivably have created new products to sustain employment for those who were laid off. Sad, but this is often the case. Managers: stay committed!

Reflect on your experiences with performance reviews; what has been your experience with various performance review systems? Do you like them? Hate them? Why and why not? What would a world class system look like in your organization?

5. INTEGRATE — CREATING MEANINGFUL COMMUNICATION PROCESSES

The first question most management teams have after creating a new *Mission, Vision and Values* statement (MVV) is, "What do we do with it?" Integrating into all aspects of your HR processes is paramount to the success of your MVV. The heart of these processes typically lies within the communication processes and employee relations materials of the organization. Since HR typically controls this function, it becomes that much easier for them to communicate the MVV statement effectively.

There are countless avenues to share and ingrain your MVVs within your organization, as well as clients and customers. These can include but are not limited to:

- Your organization's newsletter
- Your organization's website
- Brochures in the front lobby as a takeaway for visitors
- Postings in employee break and meeting rooms
- Hand copies to applicants during employment interviews
- Your organization's marketing materials
- The reverse side of your organization's business cards
- Inclusion in the packaging of all shipments

If it is important enough for the organization to include in the employee handbook, the recruitment process, the performance review process and the employee job descriptions, then it is certainly important enough to include in the above areas as well.

Several years ago I worked with an organization in which many of the employees were nervous about sharing the organization MVV's with people outside of the organization. Their fear was that the Christian overtones in the MVV statement might offend customers in the Middle East. Others were nervous that prospective employees might be offended or misinterpret our intent.

When the smoke cleared and time passed, employees started to realize that the advantages far outweighed the disadvantages; it did much more good than bad.

Ultimately, the majority of employees supported it and as a result, customers displayed a newfound confidence in us and in the integrity of the organization. The customers from the Middle East never complained and we received more compliments than complaints from applicants. I believe that is how God works. When we stand for Him unashamed, anything is possible.

What will you do? Be a difference maker! Be bold in your faith. At the end of your life, as you're walking into eternity, what will you tell God? I will say, "Father, I hope You can see I was not afraid and tried to be Your good and faithful servant."

Reflect on how you may or may not have chosen to share your MVV with your employees; How about within the community and with your customers/clients? What's holding you back?

6. INTEGRATE — CREATING SUCCESSFUL TRAINING AND DEVELOPMENT

In our final example of integration of MVV's into HR practices, we will explore Training and Development (T&D). In the past 25 years, I have watched T&D dwindle to an almost nonexistent state in most organizations. I could write a book on the impact of not investing in the development of your people, but you might find it boring. It is what it is, and it won't change all that soon, unfortunately. As leaders of organizations we must decide how we are going to right ourselves and guide our employees to work in alignment with our Missions, strive for our Visions, and operate within our organizational Values.

Here are a few steps you can take to ensure you are addressing the T&D needs of your organization without going overboard:

- Discover what is needed
- Define what needs to be addressed
- Seek the resources to accomplish the T&D
- Initiate the T&D
- Follow up to ensure it was worth the investment

Discover what is needed.

Do some basic fact-finding and discover the gaps within your organization. Simply going through a job description review project can help you discover what skills and abilities are lacking in your team. Summarize these by category and you will discover trends across your organization. Take it even further and include a development aspect to your performance review process, documenting the development needs for each of your employees. When you couple this with rewriting your organization's job descriptions, you will take it to a greater, more desirable level of detail.

Define what needs to be addressed.

Without a good outline of what gap(s) needs to be closed, you have the potential to be scattered all over the place. Take the list of items that you captured during your assessment stage and better define what is needed. Employees stating they need "communication training" is just too broad. Do they need public speaking classes? Would they benefit from e-mail etiquette guidelines? Or is it interpersonal conflict resolution training that is needed? Using the term "communication training" paints in overly broad strokes.

Seek the resources to accomplish the T&D.

I am not generally an advocate of online training. While it may be good for some, I do not believe it is effective for the majority of employees. My experiences have demonstrated that people learn best when there is real interaction. There is more than one way to develop and train an employee. For years it has been customary to send people to seminars. That just does not happen much anymore.

Think outside the box.

A few years back I was supporting a organization that tragically allowed many immigrants to work for them without the benefit of English as a Second Language training for several years. When I discovered this, I was outraged that these employees were never given the resources to better themselves. When the gap was discovered, I identified a resource and hired a gentleman who had recently returned from Asia and who had been immersed in this same immigrant culture. He developed a curriculum to deliver and helped these folks learn English for less than $1,500. Now, that is what building a 'Kingdom Minded" organization is about. Don't ignore the needs of your employees!

Follow up to ensure it was worth the investment.

Another creative solution to a problem such as this is tasking an employee to become a trainer within an organization. That employee can then deliver a topic that is relevant to the need that was discovered. One organization was lacking financial management skills within the organization's leadership. The American Management Association's program, Finance for Non-Financial Managers, was delivered by an HR leader. Doing it in this fashion saved the organization tens of thousands of dollars by avoiding sending managers out to seminars and also allowing the customization of the materials.

Was it worth the investment? The CEO said it was.

The CEO in this case witnessed an increase in the attention to detail of certain executives, an embrace of principles not so easily understood before, and it also gave him insight as to who were the "A" players versus who were the "C" players.

You're probably wondering by now how this all fits into the integration of your organization's Training and Development and its relation to the MVVs of the organization. I believe it dovetails, such as in the example of the Asian immigrant employees.

When you honor your employees by developing them, they will honor you.

When you honor your employees by training them, they will honor you by giving their best for the organization. When God is reflected in your heart and the way you respect your employees by not only paying them correctly and protecting them with benefits, but truly caring about their development, your employees will see Christ in you.

Don't look the other way when it comes to T&D. Your employees will see you in a whole different way.

Reflect on what training and development programs you worked with that were successful. Why were they successful? Were they successful alone or were changes made to improve them?

Wrapping It Up

The past few chapters have given you plenty of ideas for integrating your MVV into the culture of your organization through your HR practices. There is a lot to digest, especially if you are not an HR practitioner. Don't be overwhelmed by the possibilities before you. Simply work out a plan with your team.

The first step is to create your *Mission, Vision, and Values.* Always include your employees in the process. Hire a good facilitator if necessary, but get this done for the sake of your organization.

The second step is to document what HR practices you currently have in place and what practices you still need. This may be a good time to bring in an HR expert who will, at minimum, consult with you to help you understand what practices would serve your organization best.

My firm specializes in conducting a thorough examination through a rigorous HR assessment. Contact us today if you are interested in powering your organization to the next levels of performance through the development of HR practices that drive your Mission and support your Vision in a way that personifies your wonderful Christian values.

CLOSING THOUGHTS

Family-owned organizations, as well as non-profits, have a distinct advantage over their secular counterparts. This advantage is the flexibility to state where they are coming from and how and why they are founded, without being accused of proselytizing in the workplace. Simply stating that your organization is "founded on Christian principles" will let the public know where you are coming from and will clear the air that you are not requiring your employees to commit to a certain faith's principles.

We all have choices to make as leaders. We can choose to leave behind a legacy that our families, employees, and communities can remember, or we can take an easier route, put our heads down, and reflect the politically correct agenda to which we have all been assimilated. The decision is yours and yours alone. Of course, the Holy Spirit has a lot to do with it, and I am confident that when you consult with Him, you will choose the right path — the right path to avoid worrying about sharing your faith through your MVV with your employees, community, customers, and vendors.

Having met with hundreds of people regarding the process of building *Kingdom-Minded* organizations, one thing is for certain: many recipients of this are frightened by the thought of sharing the message of Jesus with their employees. They are even frightened at the thought of insinuating that they are believers. I try to comfort them; I try to console them; I pray with them and I pray for them. But at the end of the day, they need to make the decision for their organizations. <u>They need to decide that the message of Jesus Christ is and will always be first and foremost, ahead of their organizations and their own uncertainties.</u>

When I started my HR consulting firm in April of 2011, I too had a decision to make. I could take the easy route and mask my purpose under a secular type of business model, content to secretly connect with Christian leaders to help them develop their organizations to be *Kingdom-Minded,* or I could step out in faith and "out" myself as a Christ follower to my world of secular business associates. Having friends and contacts in senior level positions at some of the most politically correct organizations in the world made me understandably nervous about how they would perceive the path I had chosen to take. Some of these executives are at such organizations as Pepsi, Merck, Kodak, Armstrong, PayChex — the list goes on. Although most of what I do does not fit within these organizations, many of these specific executives have helped by connecting me to Christian-minded business people who could help prosper my business.

Ultimately, I decided to "out" myself, and since then I have received incredible, gratifying, and heartfelt compliments spanning across my secular business network. What made me decide to go outward and name my firm "In HIS Name HR, Christian Business Consulting" was my reflection upon the passage of Matthew 25:14–30 *(NIV).*

"His master replied, 'Well done, good and faithful servant! You have been faithful with a few things; I will put you in charge of many things. Come and share your master's happiness!'"

So let me ask: if you were to meet God tomorrow, would you feel that you shared the message of Jesus with all whom you knew? Are you truly a good and faithful servant? I know that when the day comes, I want to be able to look in God's eyes and ask, "Father, was I pleasing? Did I honor You with my life?" I want to hear, "Well done, My good and faithful servant!"

What are you going to hear when you ask?

CONNECT WITH US ONLINE!

DISCOVER MORE WAYS TO BUILD A KINGDOM MINDED ORGANIZATION
AND
RECEIVE DAILY ENCOURAGEMENT!

Follow us on Twitter:
@InHISNameHR

Subscribe to our Blog:
InHISNameHR.com

"Like" us on Facebook:
Facebook.com/InHISNameHR

Connect with us on LinkedIn:
Linkedin.com/in/MarkAGriffin

About The Author

Mark is married to Gail, and they celebrated 25 years in marriage in 2011. Mark, Gail, and daughter Emily reside in Lancaster County, Pennsylvania with their Bichon Friese, Buster. Mark and Gail's adult son Adam lives in Harrisburg, PA.

When Mark is not working he enjoys extensive backwoods backpacking, deer hunting with Adam, frequenting the gym, and enjoying time with family and friends.

After high school, Mark served in the United States Air Force while simultaneously working on his Bachelor's degree in Human Resources Administration from Saint Leo University. Mark is proud that he finished the degree while completing his four-year commitment. He returned to Pennsylvania where he quickly entered into the MBA program at Bloomsburg University while interning for Congressmen Kanjorski as a Military Liaison during the first Gulf War.

Mark then began his career working for medium and fortune organizations. Having had a wonderful, impactful career Mark ultimately landed the position he aspired to his whole career as VP of Human Resources for an international organization.

With an extensive career in Human Resources, Mark knows the impact wrong decisions can have on an organization. He can guide you in how best to act within your values and the values of your organization.

Mark has had the pleasure of working for Christian owned organizations, and he knows what works and does not work. Most importantly he sees the world through the employees' perspective! He believes in treating everyone with dignity and respect because your employees are part of your organization family.

APPENDIX

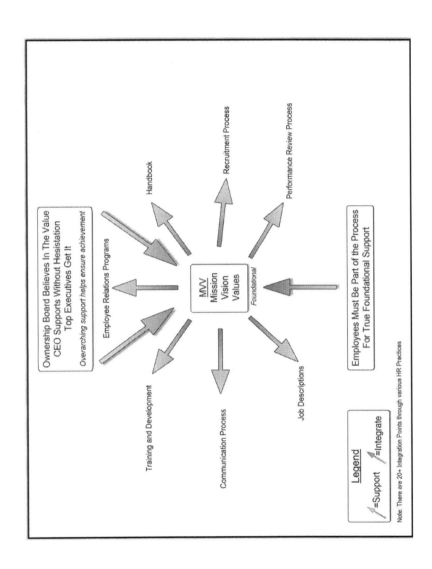

Made in the USA
Columbia, SC
10 December 2022

72507548R00041